CREATOR **Darla Hall**

Hey kids! My name is Darla Hall and I am the creator of the Go Cowboys Activity Book. I hope you enjoy all of the fun games, mazes, puzzles, dream team playing cards, stickers and activities in this book.

The idea for this book began as a gift to cheer up a little boy in the hospital. I continue donating activity books like this to children in hospitals everywhere.

To learn more about these books or purchase other team books, please visit my website at www.inthesportszone.com.

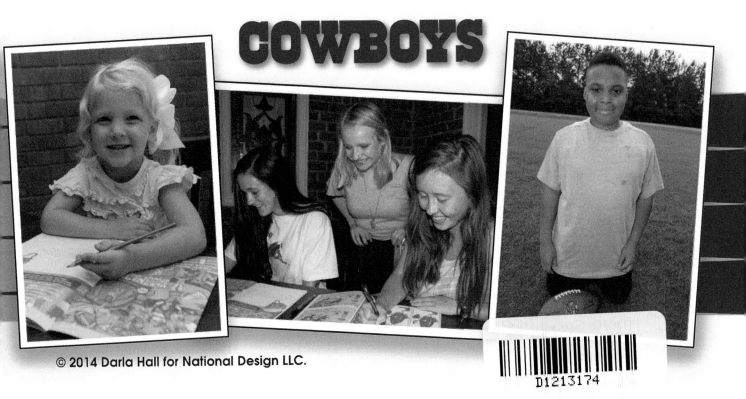

COWBOYS

D1213174

We hope you enjoy this activity book to show your team spirit.

ME

MY FAMILY

DRAW YOURSELF IN YOUR
FAVORITE TEAM GEAR

MY FRIENDS

MY FAVORITE PLAYER

COWBOYS

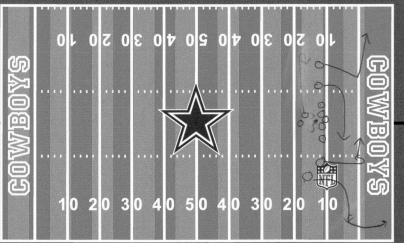

DRAW YOUR WINNING OFFENSIVE PLAY.

DRAW YOUR WINNING DEFENSIVE PLAY.

Name your team & describe your play

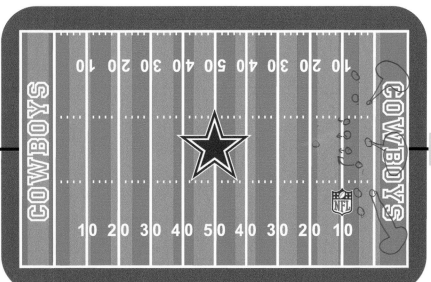

Go Cowboys

COWBOYS

COWBOYS

What would your Cowboys mascot look like?

IF YOU COULD CREATE YOUR OWN MASCOT, WHAT WOULD IT LOOK LIKE?

EVEN IF YOUR TEAM ALREADY HAS A MASCOT, USE YOUR MOST CREATIVE IDEAS TO CREATE A ONE OF A KIND MASCOT.

BE CREATIVE! HAVE FUN!

The Cowboys tailgate party needs your help

BUILD A BLAZIN' TAILGATE CAMPFIRE!

COWBOYS

Yum! Yum!

I think the offensive and defensive lines eat this for a snack. Add food to the table.

COWBOYS

COWBOYS

THERE ARE NOT MANY
FANS IN THE STANDS YET.
YOU CAN CHANGE THAT
BY DRAWING THEM IN.
GET CREATIVE!

TIC-TAC-GO COWBOYS-TOE

Word Scramblers

BYWSOOC
1. _____

SCOAMT
2. _____

ROTNADTII
3. _____

HCMSOAPIN
4. _____

LBOOFTAL
5. _____

MSTUAID
6. _____

YLEPATN
7. _____

KRCKEI
8. _____

AQBRTURAECK
9. _____

HELP RUSHER GET TO THE GAME -

START HERE

FINISH HERE

AT THE FOOTBALL STADIUM!

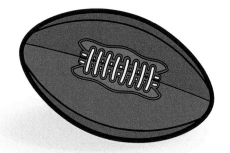

COWBOYS

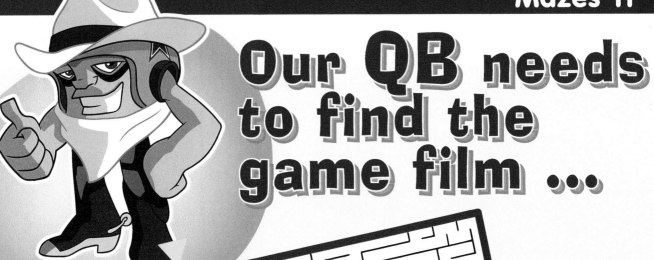

Our QB needs to find the game film ...

help him so we can scout the opponent!

HURRY ! FANS ARE ANXIOUS TO GET TO PARTICIPATE IN NFL PLAY 60 ACTIVITIES !

Fact: About NFL Play 60

Our Mission: To make the next generation of youth the most active and healthy.
In October 2007, the NFL launched NFL PLAY 60, a national youth health and fitness campaign focused on increasing the wellness of young fans by encouraging them to be active for at least 60 minutes a day.

Designed to tackle childhood obesity, NFL PLAY 60 brings together the NFL's long-standing commitment to health and fitness with an impressive roster of partner organizations. In addition to national outreach and online programs, NFL PLAY 60 is implemented at the grassroots level through NFL's in-school, after-school and team-based programs. The NFL PLAY 60 initiative is prominent during the NFL's key calendar events, including Super Bowl, Pro Bowl, Draft, Kickoff and Thanksgiving and is supported by many NFL players and coaches year round. To date, the NFL has dedicated over $200 million to youth health and wellness through NFL PLAY 60.

Dream Big. Play Big.

There are many ways you can join the PLAY 60 movement. You can get involved through school programs, contests and community events.

COWBOYS

FOOTBALL FACTS

HOW WELL DO YOU KNOW THE GAME OF FOOTBALL?

ACROSS

3. AN OFFICIAL THROWS THIS TO SIGNAL A PENALTY
5. AN EXTRA _____ IS WORTH 1 POINT
6. THIS PLAYER STARTS THE PLAYS
7. THE FIRST FOOTBALL WAS THIS SHAPE
8. PLAYERS ARE ASSIGNED THESE TO REPRESENT THEIR POSITIONS
10. THIS CAN BE TURF OR REAL GRASS

DOWN

1. THE END ZONE IS THIS MANY YARDS
2. WHEN A TEAM SCORES 6 POINTS
4. A FIELD ____ IS WORTH 3 POINTS
9. NUMBER OF PLAYERS ON THE FIELD PLAYING AT ONE TIME

COLOR YOUR
RUSH ZONE
CHARACTER

You are a WINNER

CREATE YOUR OWN MEDALS

COWBOYS

THE COWBOYS FOOTBALL TEAM NEEDS YOUR SUPPORT.

CREATE A RALLY SIGN THAT YOU CAN HOLD UP AT THE NEXT GAME TO CHEER ON YOUR TEAM.

COWBOYS

FUN FOOTBALL FACTS

- Footballs used to be made out of pigskin. Now they are made from other materials.
- The first official rules for football were written in 1876.
- Each team has 11 players on the field at one time.

FOOTBALL GLOSSARY

Center - the person who snaps the ball to the quarterback.

Defense - the team trying to stop the other team from scoring.

Offense - the team that has the ball.

Punt - to kick the ball to the other team when you have not been able to gain 10 yards in three downs.

Tackle - to pull a person to the ground.

Football Fun Facts

18 NFL Trivia

NORTH/SOUTH/EAST/WEST

 A

DIVISION TRIVIA

 N

AMERICAN FOOTBALL CONFERENCE

AFC NORTH TEAMS

10 BALTIMORE RAVENS

 CINCINNATI BENGALS

CLEVELAND BROWNS

2 PITTSBURGH STEELERS

AFC SOUTH TEAMS

 HOUSTON TEXANS

11 INDIANAPOLIS COLTS

 JACKSONVILLE JAGUARS

 TENNESSEE TITANS

AFC EAST TEAMS

 BUFFALO BILLS

12 MIAMI DOLPHINS

3 NEW ENGLAND PATRIOTS

 NEW YORK JETS

AFC WEST TEAMS

8 DENVER BRONCOS

 KANSAS CITY CHIEFS

9 OAKLAND RAIDERS

SAN DIEGO CHARGERS

NATIONAL FOOTBALL CONFERENCE

NFC NORTH TEAMS

13 CHICAGO BEARS

 DETROIT LIONS

5 GREEN BAY PACKERS

14 MINNESOTA VIKINGS

NFC SOUTH TEAMS

 ATLANTA FALCONS

 CAROLINA PANTHERS

 NEW ORLEANS SAINTS

 TAMPA BAY BUCCANEERS

NFC EAST TEAMS

1 DALLAS COWBOYS

6 NEW YORK GIANTS

 PHILADELPHIA EAGLES

7 WASHINGTON REDSKINS

NFC WEST TEAMS

 ARIZONA CARDINALS

4 SAN FRANCISCO 49ers

 SEATTLE SEAHAWKS

15 LOS ANGELES RAMS

USING THE CHART ABOVE, ANSWER THE FOLLOWING QUESTIONS:

1. Are the Cowboys in the American or National Conference? NFC

2. What division are they in? NFC East

3. What three other teams are in their division? Giants/skins/eagle

4. Name one team in the AFC South. Texans

5. How many teams are there in the NFL? 32

Go Cowboys - Offense

Here is your chance to create your own Cowboys Dream Team. Use these player cards to create a winning offense or defense. Or you can mix & match. There are no rules. See how your team stacks up against others. Use your imagination and make up your own stats for each player or search the Internet for their actual stats. Have fun with it!

Name Troy Aikman
Position QB
Height   Weight
Hometown
History/Stats   HOF, MVP

Name Emmitt Smith
Position RB
Height   Weight
Hometown
History/Stats

Name Michael Irvin
Position
Height   Weight
Hometown
History/Stats

Name
Position
Height   Weight
Hometown
History/Stats

Name
Position
Height   Weight
Hometown
History/Stats

Name
Position
Height   Weight
Hometown
History/Stats

Name
Position
Height   Weight
Hometown
History/Stats

Name
Position
Height   Weight
Hometown
History/Stats

Name
Position
Height   Weight
Hometown
History/Stats

Name
Position
Height   Weight
Hometown
History/Stats

Name
Position
Height   Weight
Hometown
History/Stats

Go Cowboys - Offense

Name _____
Position _____
Height _____ Weight _____
Hometown _____
History/Stats _____

Name _____
Position _____
Height _____ Weight _____
Hometown _____
History/Stats _____

Name _____
Position _____
Height _____ Weight _____
Hometown _____
History/Stats _____

Name _____
Position _____
Height _____ Weight _____
Hometown _____
History/Stats _____

Name _____
Position _____
Height _____ Weight _____
Hometown _____
History/Stats _____

Name _____
Position _____
Height _____ Weight _____
Hometown _____
History/Stats _____

Name _____
Position _____
Height _____ Weight _____
Hometown _____
History/Stats _____

Name _____
Position _____
Height _____ Weight _____
Hometown _____
History/Stats _____

Name _____
Position _____
Height _____ Weight _____
Hometown _____
History/Stats _____

Name _____
Position _____
Height _____ Weight _____
Hometown _____
History/Stats _____

Name _____
Position _____
Height _____ Weight _____
Hometown _____
History/Stats _____

GO COWBOYS

FOOTBALL

Go Cowboys - Defense

Go Cowboys - Defense

raw yourself performing your favorite team song.

COWBOYS

COWBOYS

GO COWBOYS

NFL

ACTIVITIES

GO COWBOYS

NFL

ACTIVITIES

COWBOYS

NFL

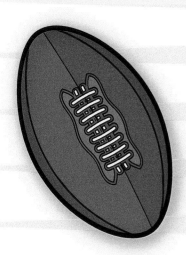

It's time to set up your Cowboys tailgate part

Add your favorite foods, friends, toys, chairs, games, tables, and more! Use your imagination!

COWBOYS GAME SCHEDULE

Date	Game	Location	Result	W	L

COWBOYS **NFL**

GAME STATS:

TRDFA

PELSYAR

SAHCEOC

WESRON

KIPC

CERRATK

SEORPPCT

LEATSS

SPDORNIECIT

TAESM

RONDU

SLSAC

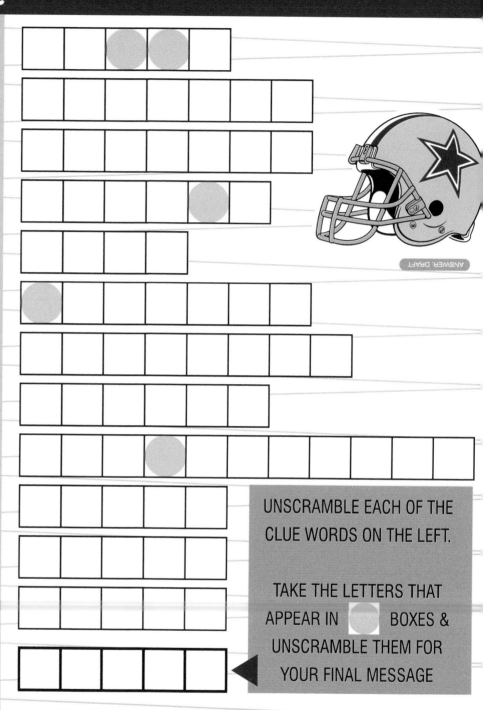

ANSWER: DRAFT

UNSCRAMBLE EACH OF THE CLUE WORDS ON THE LEFT.

TAKE THE LETTERS THAT APPEAR IN ⬤ BOXES & UNSCRAMBLE THEM FOR YOUR FINAL MESSAGE

NFL DRAFT

COWBOYS

NFL RUSH

www.nflrush.com

The official NFL site for kids.
Your source for fun NFL online games, contests,
fantasy football, youth football, and NFL Play 60.

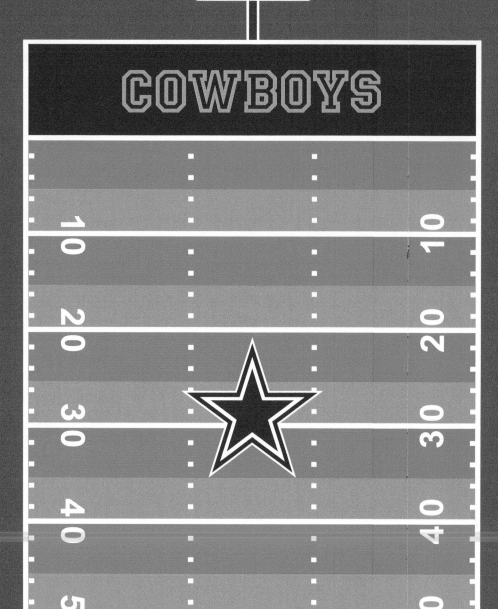

HOW TO PLAY
TAILGATE TABLE SLIDE

The object of the game is to get more points than your opponent.
Play is simple; you slide a Quarter up the field by using the palm of your hand. You position the coin on the bottom edge of the playing field and with the palm tap at it, making it slide up the field. You need to get the first coin between the 50 - 40 yard lines to gain points and so up the field. If you are on a line you can use your second and third coin to play off the first coin to move it between the line. When you have moved a coin in between the lines, mark it on the side of the field. First player to score between all yard lines can then play for a touchdown to win the game.

Or, you can make up your own game using the football field.
Be creative & have hours of fun...

HOW TO SET UP YOUR
TAILGATE TABLE SLIDE.

1. Cut out the page then fold the bottom of the page where shown.

2. Place the playing field against the edge of a table or flat surface & you are set to play.

3. Each player will need 3 Quarters as a ball to play with.

FOLD HERE

COWBOYS

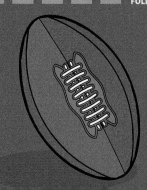

X

SCORES
COWBOYS
V

X
_____

X

SCORES
COWBOYS
V

X
_____

X

SCORES
COWBOYS
V

X
_____

X

SCORES
COWBOYS
V

X
_____

X

SCORES
COWBOYS
V

X
_____

WINNER'S NAME

WINNER'S NAME

WINNER'S NAME

WINNER'S NAME

WINNER'S NAME

COWBOYS

HOW TO PLAY NFL BINGO

PREPARE: Cut out the symbols and put the squares into a hat or bowl.

DISTRIBUTE: Use the two Bingo Cards on this page.

CALL: The caller should pull out one image, describe it and show it to the players.

MARK IMAGE: The player will then place pennies, rocks, or something similar on the called image if it is on your card.

WINNING: Once a predetermined pattern is made on a card, the player with that card calls out -

NFL BINGO!

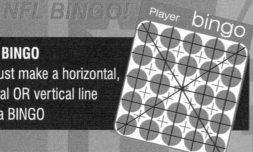

LINES BINGO
You must make a horizontal, diagonal OR vertical line to get a BINGO

Player 1 bingo

Player 2 bingo

Connect the dots

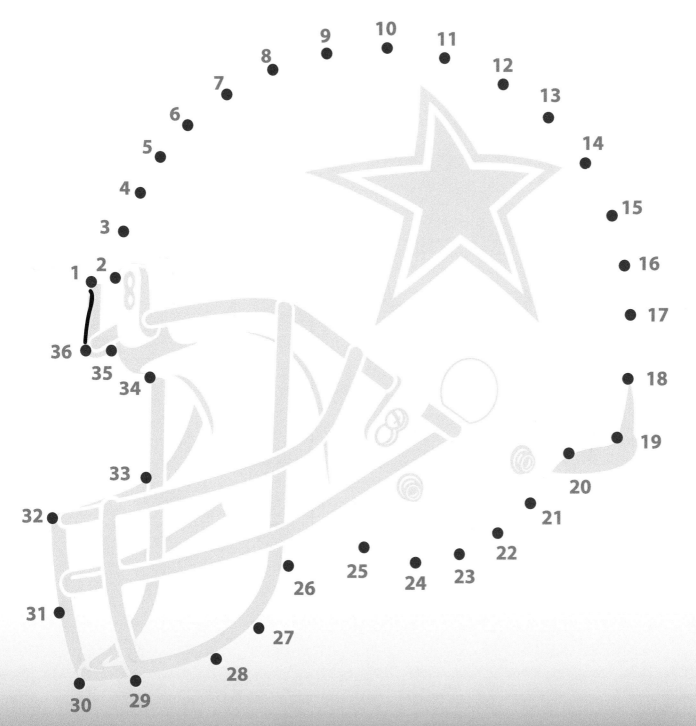

COWBOYS

Connect the dots

Get in the spirit of the game!
Use this to yell loud & proud.

COWBOYS

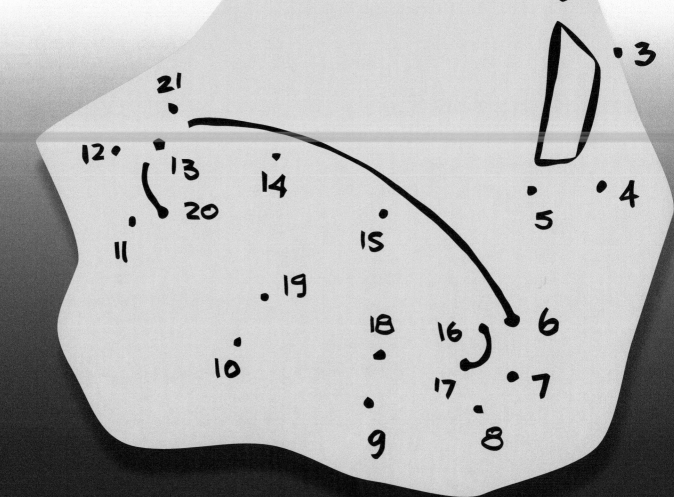

FOOTBALL TRIVIA

1. WHAT WERE FOOTBALLS ORIGINALLY MADE OUT OF?

   _____

2. WHAT YEAR WERE THE FIRST OFFICIAL RULES FOR FOOTBALL WRITTEN?

   _____

3. HOW MANY PLAYERS DOES EACH TEAM HAVE ON THE FIELD PLAYING AT ONE TIME?

   __ll_____

4. WHO IS THE PERSON WHO SNAPS THE BALL TO THE QUARTERBACK?

   _center_____

5. WHO KICKS THE BALL TO THE OTHER TEAM WHEN YOU HAVE NOT BEEN ABLE TO GAIN 10 YARDS IN THREE DOWNS?

   _Punter_____

6. HOW MANY YARDS IS THE LENGTH OF A REGULATION FOOTBALL FIELD?

   _120_____

7. WHERE IS THE PRO FOOTBALL HALL OF FAME?

   _Canton_____

8. HOW MANY POINTS DO YOU RECEIVE FOR A TOUCHDOWN?

   _6_____

Answers on page 41

CAN YOU FIND 5 DIFFERENCES IN THESE PICTURES?

CAN YOU FIND 10 DIFFERENCES IN THESE PICTURES?

AWARDS	BLITZ	CENTER
DEFENSE	FIELD	FLY
FOOTBALL	GAME	HALFBACK
KICKER	LINEBACKER	LOSSES
OFFENSE	PASS	PLAYER
POINTS	POSITION	PUNTER
QUARTERBACK	RUN	SAFETY
SCRIMMAGE	SWEEP	
WINS	TOUCHDOWN	

DHU ÖVÂ MPUK ÄOLZL ÉVYKZ HZZVJPHÄLK ÉPÄO ÄOL NHTL VM MVVÄIHSS?

```
O N R P A E P J L E C F A D Q
F W E E T B G O J P L S W U E
F O Y E C Z S A S Y K L A W V
E D A W J S T P M I X R R N S
N H L S E I D I N M T M D C W
S C P S A E Z S L E I I S U J
E U W N F B N L R B S R O E Z
J O R E K C A B E N I L C N O
R T N Y S B A R E K C I K S P
O S P S T C H A L F B A C K R
E B A O K E D L E I F N I E U
K P O H I O F G A M E W T N B
D F R A N N F A Q Y X N I X A
O P U D P G T Q S J E I E N Y
P U N T E R F S P C A N K Q S
```

COWBOYS

GO COWBOYS

A Q E M B N G L Z C S Q P M W
V N B S Q Z X S H G N O U A X
C C N Z N E P A N V O S P F R
Z O M O M E M B U D I I G E T
X D A S U P F F F C S A D H R
H T F C I N Q E Y K S A E X A
F H U O H Z C A D M E E S V D
I G N W M P D E D L C T N K I
E S I P N E U H R K N G E N T
L W N A M V W E D O O F F T I
D U J A P N E P W Y C L F G O
Y W G K F H L L A B T O O F N
Q G R E C T A I L G A T I N G
M A S C O T Z O X Z C S I I G
E L U A N R O O O Q S C C Z F

ANNOUNCER	CHAMPIONS	CHEERLEADER
COACH	CONCESSIONS	DEFENSE
FANS	FIELD	FOOD
FOOTBALL	FUN	GAMEDAY
MASCOT	MUSIC	OFFENSE
TAILGATING	TRADITION	

COWBOYS

```
P N C Z L V T R M U H P U F S
L R W M J S E K Z E L J A J E
N T O N L E L F K A D N D C L
I E J F I L E A N P T I O S U
A A G W E D V O I A N N A T D
P M G P R S I E S C F A Q N E
R S E A D T S Y U E I O G E H
O S F R A Z I I R G M F N V C
G T A N I R O E O T A A F E S
R W F Y A C N X B N R E G O K
A K Y C D C A S E M A G L M G
M Y P H E N H N E R U L E S A
S T H G I L H G I H F V J L G
F O O T B A L L S R E Y A L P
H K G J K T G I T G J M C E A
```

AMERICAN
DRAFT
FOOTBALL
HIGHLIGHTS
NATIONAL
PROFESSIONAL
SCHEDULES
AWARDS
EVENTS
GAME
LEAGUE
OFFICIALS
PROGRAMS
TEAMS
CONFERENCE
FANTASY
MEDIA
PLAYERS
RULES
TELEVISION

COWBOYS FOOTBALL

COWBOYS
GAME ANSWERS

FOOTBALL TRIVIA ANSWERS

1) Pigskin   3) 11   5) Punter   7) Canton, Ohio

2) 1876   4) Center   6) 100 Yards   8) 6

WORD SCRAMBLE ANSWERS

BYWSOOC **COWBOYS**	HCMSOAPIN **CHAMPIONS**	YLEPATN **PENALTY**
SCOAMT **MASCOT**	LBOOFTAL **FOOTBALL**	KRCKEI **KICKER**
ROTNADTII **TRADITION**	MSTUAID **STADIUM**	AQBRTURAECK **QUARTERBACK**

SPOT THE DIFFERENCES

NFL TRIVIA ANSWERS

1. NATIONAL FOOTBALL CONFERENCE
2. NFC EAST
3. NEW YORK GIANTS / PHILADELPHIA EAGLES / WASHINGTON REDSKIN
4. TEXANS / COLTS / JAGUARS / TITANS
5. 32 TEAMS

CROSSWORD

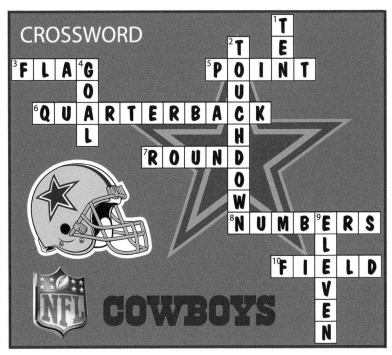

WORD SEARCH

COWBOYS FOOTBALL

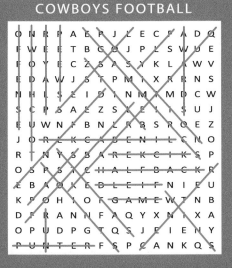

GO COWBOYS

NFL

Here is a writing prompt for you.

Your job is to finish the story. Be creative!

Don't hold back. Write as much as you can.

Use a lot of adjectives (ask an adult what

that means if you don't know).

The Dallas Cowboys' head coach retired, and you have been named as the new head coach.

Hurry, you have a news conference in 10 minutes.

What are you going to say to address the media?

What is it that you love about Dallas Cowboys football? Talk about all aspects of the game, from the coaches to the players to the tailgate to the opponents, and everything in between.

IVSK VU...
ÄOL DVÉIVÖZ
HYL JVTPUN!

ZVÂ HYL OHƇPUN H KYLHT.
ZVÂ HYL ÄOL XÂHYÄLYIHJR VM ÄOL
MVVÄIHSS ÄLHT. XOHÄ ÉVÂSK ÖVÂ KV
MVY ÖVÂY NHTL WYLWHYHÄPVU?
XVÂSK ÖVÂ OHUN VÂÂ HUK ÄHPSNHÄL HÄ
ÄOL TÄHKPÂT, KHUJL ÄV ÄOL MPNOÄ ZVUN,
WYHJÄPJL, LHÄ, OHUN VÂÂ ÉPÄO MYPLUKZ,
ÉHÄJO NHTL MPST?
XYPÄL H ZÄVYÖ HIVÂÄ ÖVÂY KHÖ PU
ÄOL SPML VM ILPUN ÄOL DPXCPZT RC.

ULSS ÂZ HIVÂÄ ÖVÂY KYLHT!

Cowboys Football Weekly

Cowboys are in the news.

Read all about it!

WHAT HAPPENS IN YOUR STORY?

_____

_____

_____

_____

_____

_____

_____

_____

History of American Football

The history of American football can be traced to early versions of rugby football and association football. Both games have their origin in varieties of football played in Britain in the mid-19th century, in which a football is kicked at a goal and/or run over a line.

WRITE ABOUT YOUR FAVORITE SPORT AND HOW IT HAS IMPACTED YOUR LIFE. WRITE ABOUT YOUR FAVORITE TEAM, PLAYERS, TRADITIONS, AND MORE!

COWBOYS

HOW MANY OF THESE ITEMS CAN YOU FIND IN THIS PICTURE?

- MUSICAL NOTES
- STARS
- GRILL
- FOOTBALL
- PIZZA SLICE
- COOLER
- CLOCK
- NFL LOGOS
- BALLOONS
- BIRDS

TIC-TAC-GO COWBOYS-TOE

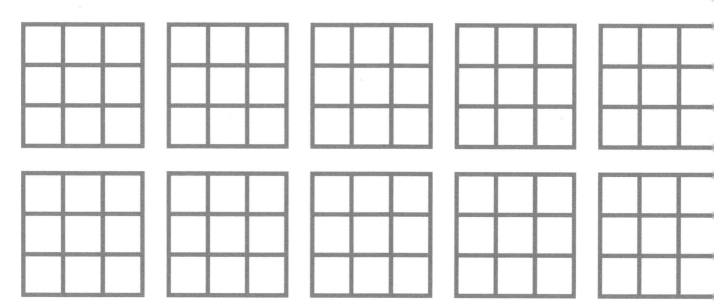

COWBOYS

COWBOYS

GO·COWBOYS

ACTIVITIES

COWBOYS

COWBOYS

COWBOYS

COWBOYS